First Facts®

CURIOUS SCIENTISTS

MIND-BLOWING PHYSICAL SCIENCE ACTIVITIES

by Angie Smibert

CAPSTONE PRESS
a capstone imprint

First Facts are published by Capstone Press,
1710 Roe Crest Drive, North Mankato, Minnesota 56003
www.mycapstone.com

Library of Congress Cataloging-in-Publication Data
Cataloging-in-publication information is on file with the Library of Congress.
ISBN 978-1-5157-6887-6 (library binding)
ISBN 978-1-5157-6893-7 (paperback)
ISBN 978-1-5157-6905-7 (eBook PDF)

Editorial Credits
Anna Butzer, editor; Heidi Thompson, designer; Morgan Walters, media researcher; Laura Manthe, production specialist

Photo Credits
All photos are shot by the Capstone Studio, Karon Dubke

Artistic Elements
Shutterstock: amgun, (gears) design element throughout

Printed and bound in the USA.
010374F17

TABLE OF CONTENTS

STAY CURIOUS

Do you wonder how things work? When you look at a helicopter, do you wonder what parts make it fly? Can something be both a liquid and a solid? To find out the answers to questions like these, curious scientists do experiments.

Now it's your turn to be a curious scientist. Get ready to use your creativity and get a little messy! You'll experiment with magnetism, **electricity**, and **gravity**. You will bend water, get slimy, and more. The results of your experiments might just blow your mind!

Safe Science

Read through each activity before starting. Collect all of the materials that you will need. You may need an adult to help you find or buy some materials. Experiments can be tricky. Be sure to ask an adult for help if you need it.

electricity— flow or stream of charged particles, such as electrons

gravity—a force that pulls objects with mass together; gravity pulls objects down toward the center of Earth

LAVA LAMP

Have you ever seen a lava lamp? Blobs of colors float around in a clear liquid. The colored blobs and the liquid don't mix. They have different **densities**. The blobs are lighter, so they float. You can create your own lava lamp using a few common household items.

Materials:

- clear plastic bottle with lid
- vegetable oil
- water
- food coloring
- antacid tablets

Steps:

1. Fill the bottle about three-fourths full with vegetable oil.
2. Add 5-10 drops of your favorite color.
3. Fill the rest of the bottle with water. Watch what happens. Do the oil and water mix? Which one is on top?

4. Break an antacid tablet into pieces.
5. Drop the pieces one at a time into the liquid and watch the show! You can add more tablets to keep the lava lamp going.

Tip: You can save your lava lamp and use it again. After the antacid tablets stop fizzing, put the cap on the bottle. To see the lava action again, just add more antacid pieces!

How it Works:

Just like in a real lava lamp, the two liquids — oil and water — don't mix. One liquid is more dense than the other. The denser liquid sinks down to the bottom of the bottle. The antacid tablets release a gas when they hit the water. The gas is lighter. Its bubbles float to the top. Some of the bubbles capture the food coloring drops and take them for a ride.

The lava lamp was invented in 1963. In the real lamp, colored wax floats in a liquid. A light bulb melts the wax. This makes it less dense than the liquid.

density—the amount of mass an object or substance has based on a unit of volume

MAGNETIC SLIME

Magnets attract metal. If you hold a strong magnet over a pile of paper clips they will hop up to meet it. But what about slime? It's sort of solid and sort of liquid, but it is not metal. Can you make slime ooze toward a magnet? Let's find out!

Materials:

- 2 bowls
- white or clear craft glue, 4 oz bottle or ½ cup (113 grams)
- water
- 1 teaspoon Borax powder
- measuring cup
- craft sticks for stirring
- 3 tablespoons magnetic powder (black ferric oxide powder or iron filings)
- strong magnet (Rare-earth or neodymium magnets work best.)

Steps:

1. Pour the glue into one bowl.
2. Add an equal amount of water.
3. Stir until the glue and water are mixed.
4. In the other bowl, add 1 teaspoon of the Borax powder and 1 cup of water. Stir until the Borax dissolves.
5. Slowly stir the Borax **solution** into the bowl with the glue until the slime begins to form. Knead the slime with your hands.
6. Sprinkle in the **magnetic** powder.

Tip: Fill the now empty glue bottle with water.

Step 3

7. Knead the slime again until the powder is mixed all the way through the slime.

8. Now you're ready to experiment with the magnet. Place the magnet next to the slime on a smooth surface and watch. The slime should ooze over to the magnet and swallow it up.

Tip: You can store your slime in a sandwich bag or plastic container with a lid.

Step 7

How it Works:

What's going on here? Two things are actually happening. First, when you mix the Borax and glue together, the glue goes through a chemical change. The glue begins to stick to itself — instead of other things.

Second, the powder you mixed into the slime contains iron. Metals such as iron, steel, nickel, and cobalt are attracted to magnets. The magnet creates a **magnetic field**. This is a space around the magnet where it pulls (or pushes). So when the slime gets close enough to the magnetic field, it pulls the iron in the slime toward the magnet.

solution—a liquid in which one or more substances are dissolved

magnetic— having the attractive properties of a magnet

magnetic field—region around a magnetic material or a moving electric charge within which the force of magnetism acts

RUBBER EGG BOUNCE

What happens when you drop a raw egg? Splat, right? What if you could make an egg bounce? In this experiment you will turn a raw egg into a rubber one. Then you can see how gravity acts on it.

Materials:

- raw egg, in the shell
- plastic cup or container
- white vinegar
- ruler or tape measure

Steps:

1. Put the egg in the cup or container.
2. Fill the cup with enough vinegar to cover the egg. Notice any bubbles rising?
3. Wait at least 24 hours. The shell should dissolve. The egg should have a rubbery yellow covering on it.
4. Take the egg out of the vinegar. You can gently peel off any remaining bits of shell.
5. Now it's time to experiment with bouncing the egg! Go outside or somewhere you can make a mess. Start just an inch or two above the ground or surface. Gently drop the egg. What happens? Try dropping it from a little higher. At what height does the egg break?

Step 2

How it Works:

The eggshell undergoes a chemical change. The acid in the vinegar dissolves the calcium carbonate in the eggshell. The bubbles you saw are carbon dioxide gas escaping as the shell dissolves. This leaves just the membrane holding the egg together. The vinegar doesn't dissolve it. The vinegar makes the membrane tougher. Under the membrane, the egg white and yolk are still liquid. The membrane can withstand more force, but it will eventually break. The higher you drop the egg, the more force it hits the ground with — until splat! Experiment with leaving the egg in the vinegar longer. Can it withstand more force?

Step 3

BENDING WATER

Have you ever shuffled your feet across a rug and then touched a doorknob? What happened? You got zapped, right? That zap was **static electricity**. In this experiment you will harness static electricity to bend water.

Materials:

- balloon
- faucet
- hair, clean and dry

Steps:

1. Blow up the balloon.
2. Turn on the faucet so there's just a thin stream of water coming out.
3. Rub the balloon against your hair about 10 times.
4. Slowly hold the balloon closer and closer to the trickle of water — without touching it.
5. The stream of water should bend toward the balloon!
6. Now repeat the experiment with other objects. For example, can you use static electricity to pull a sheet of paper toward you?

static electricity—electricity that collects on the surface of an object

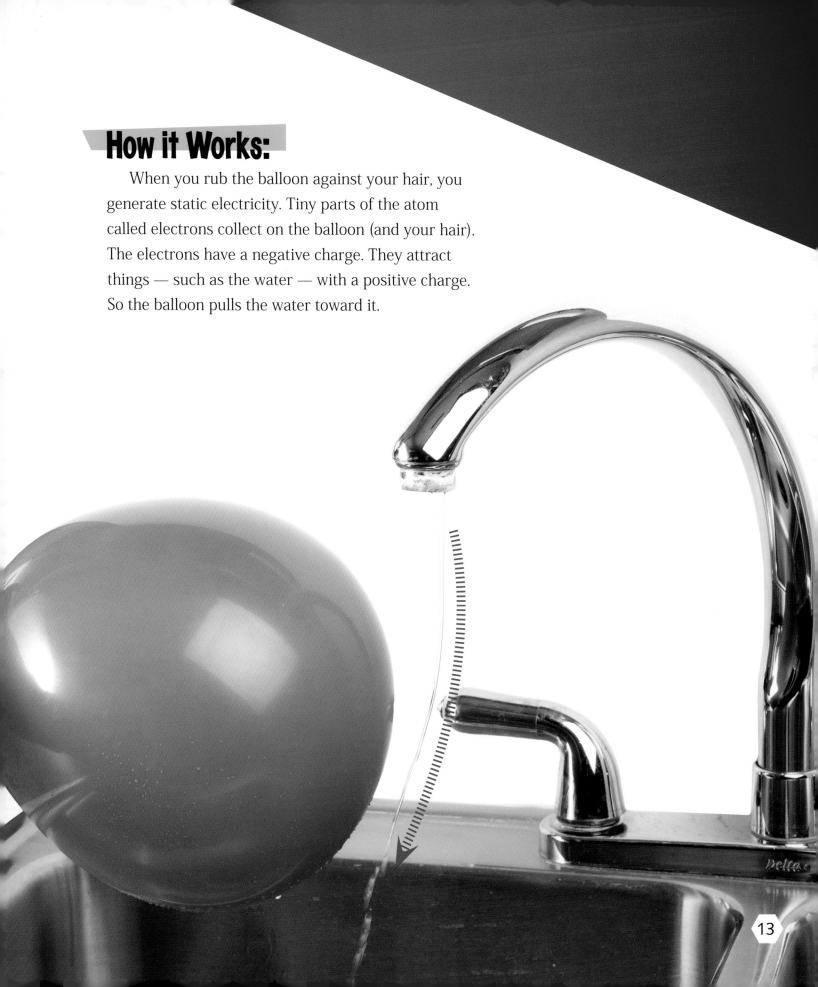

How it Works:

When you rub the balloon against your hair, you generate static electricity. Tiny parts of the atom called electrons collect on the balloon (and your hair). The electrons have a negative charge. They attract things — such as the water — with a positive charge. So the balloon pulls the water toward it.

EASY HERO'S ENGINE

Most **engines** work the same way. A force pushes the car or rocket. The force comes from burning gas, exploding rocket fuel, or electricity. But you don't need any of those to make this engine. It runs on gravity and water.

Materials:

- string, 5-6 inches (12.7-15.2 centimeters)
- plastic soda or water bottle with a cap
- craft knife
- small metal nut
- duct tape
- 2 plastic bendy straws
- water

Step 1

Steps:

1. Ask an adult to help you poke a hole in the top of the cap. Pull the string through and tie the nut onto the end.
2. Ask an adult to poke two holes on opposite sides of the water bottle. These holes should be near the bottom of the bottle. They should be just a little bigger than the straws.
3. Trim each straw 1 to 2 inches (2.5 to 5 cm) below the bendable part. (If you use a bigger bottle, you may want a longer straw.)
4. Slide a straw into each hole. Cover any gaps between the bottle and straw with tape.
5. Bend the straws so that they're L shaped. Point each straw in the opposite direction.

Step 5

6. Take your bottle outside or hold it over a sink. Fill the bottle with water and quickly screw on the cap.
7. Lift the bottle by the string and watch what happens. (It should spin.)
8. Experiment with pointing the ends of the straws in different directions.

How it Works:

Gravity pulls the water down and out each straw. Every force has an equal and opposite reaction. So the force of the water pushes the bottle in the opposite direction. This makes the bottle spin.

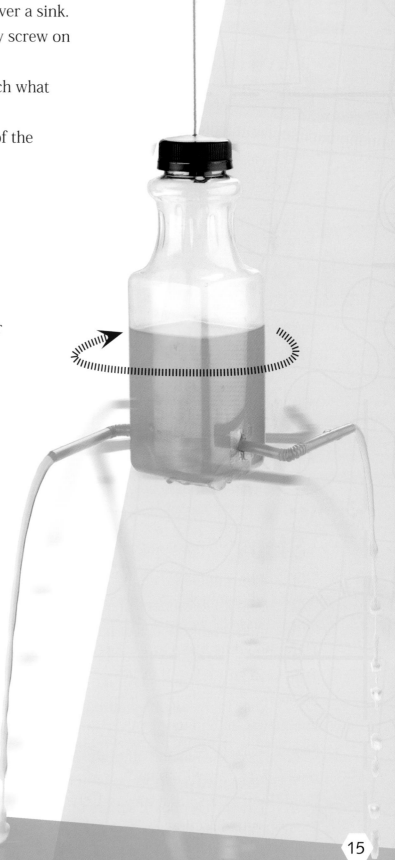

The Real Hero's Engine

In the 1st century AD, Hero of Alexandria invented the first steam engine. It was a round copper container with L-shaped tubes. When the water inside the container was heated, the steam escaped from the tubes, causing the container to spin.

engine—a machine that makes the power needed to move something

SPLATTER PATTERNS

Water balloons are cool fun on a hot day. But they can also be creative science! What happens when you drop a paint-filled balloon from different heights? In this experiment you are going to find out, and make some awesome art. Time to get messy! You'll need to do this experiment outside!

Materials:

- empty plastic water bottle
- funnel
- washable craft paint (3 colors)
- corn starch
- water (from hose or tap)
- 3 water balloons
- 5- x 5- inch (12.7- x 12.7- cm) cardboard square
- adhesive putty
- 3 thumbtacks

Steps:

1. Put funnel into empty plastic water bottle.
2. Add 2 tablespoons of corn starch to water bottle.
3. Add 3 tablespoons of paint to water bottle.
4. Add 1/2 cup (235 milliliters) water to water bottle.
5. Put cap on and shake it up. Blow water balloon up a few times to stretch it out. Take cap off water bottle and put the water balloon over the opening. Tip bottle upside down and squeeze the paint water into the balloon.
6. Take the balloon off of the water bottle and tie it off.
7. Repeat steps 1 through 3 for the rest of the balloons.
8. Lay the cardboard square on a flat surface outside.

9. Put 3 balls of adhesive putty in the middle of the cardboard. Place the thumbtacks pointy side up in the middle of the putty. This will help break the balloons.

10. Drop the first balloon from shoulder height. How big of a splatter did it make?

11. Drop the second balloon from waist height. How big is this splash?

12. Drop the third balloon from knee height.

Which balloon had the biggest splash? Did you notice a pattern? Experiment by dropping balloons from even higher places.

How it Works:

The higher balloons should have made the bigger splatters. When you let go of the balloon, gravity is the force that pulls it to the ground. But the balloon also has something called **potential energy**. As you hold it above the ground, the balloon has the potential to release energy. The higher the balloon is, the more potential energy it has. So the higher object will hit the ground with more energy.

potential energy—energy stored within an object, waiting to be released

MINI-MOTOR

In a car, the motor makes the axles spin. This helps move the vehicle. Other machines have motors that make some parts move. Most motors run on either electricity or gas. In this experiment, you'll get to create a simple electrical motor — and watch it spin your copper artwork!

Materials:

- AA battery
- neodymium magnet
- copper wire, 5-6 inches (12.7-15.2 cm), depending on your design
- pliers or wire cutters

Steps:

1. Stack the battery on top of the magnet.
2. Bend the copper wire into a heart shape. To do that, bend the wire in half and make a small dip in the middle. Keep the bottom of the heart open.
3. Balance the dip on the top of the battery.
4. Bend the ends of the wire so they curve around the magnets. The ends of the wire shouldn't touch.
5. The wire should start spinning. If it doesn't, you may need to play with the balance of the heart.
6. Experiment with different shapes. For instance, try a spiral. The top of the wire should touch the battery terminal, and the bottom should wrap around the magnet.

Step 2

How it Works:

Magnetism and electricity work together in weird and wonderful ways. Electricity flows from the battery through the copper wire. The **current** creates a magnetic field. The magnet also has one. One magnetic field pushes the other. The copper wire spins!

The homopolar motor was the first electric motor. Michael Faraday built one in 1821. He used a chemical battery to make a wire rotate. It spun over a magnet placed in a pool of mercury.

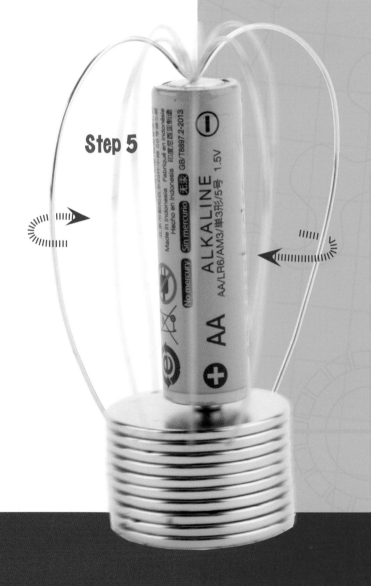

Step 5

current—the flow of electrons

INSTANT ICE

This experiment is simple but it will amaze your friends. With a flick of a finger, you can turn a bottle of water into ice! Or you can even make an instant tower of slush. The secret is super cooling.

Materials:

- 4 cups (960ml) of crushed ice
- kosher or rock salt
- bowl
- plastic bottle of purified water (16 ounce unopened works best)
- thermometer

Safety Tip:
Do not use a glass bottle! The bottle could shatter.

Steps:

1. Pour the ice and a 1/2 cup (160 g) of salt into the bowl.
2. Stick the bottle of water deep into the ice.
3. Put the thermometer in the ice near the bottle.
4. When the temperature reaches about 17°F (-8°C), take the bottle out carefully. The water should look clear and unfrozen.
5. Tap the bottle firmly with your finger.
6. The water should freeze instantly!
7. Repeat the experiment. This time don't tap the bottle. Open it carefully and then pour the water onto the ice in the bowl. What happens? The water should instantly freeze into a column of slush!

How it Works:

The freezing point of water is 32°F (0°C). Salt lowers the **freezing point**. This means the ice and the water in the bottle can get much colder. But the **super cooled** water doesn't freeze yet because it's pure. Ice crystals need something to form around. That can be a tiny speck of dirt, the surface of the bottle, or another ice crystal.

Tip: Be patient. This might not work the first time you try it.

freezing point— the temperature at which a liquid turns into a solid when cooled

super cool—to chill a liquid below its freezing point without it becoming solid

GLOSSARY

current (KUHR-uhnt)—the flow of electrons

density (DEN-si-tee)—the amount of mass an object or substance has based on a unit of volume

electricity (i-lek-TRISS-uh-tee)—flow or stream of charged particles, such as electrons

engine (EN-juhn)—a machine that makes the power needed to move something

freezing point (FREEZ-ing POYNT)—the temperature at which a liquid turns into a solid when cooled

gravity (GRAV-uh-tee)—a force that pulls objects with mass together; gravity pulls objects down toward the center of Earth.

magnetic (mag-NET-ik)—having the attractive properties of a magnet

magnetic field (mag-NET-ic FEELD)—region around a magnetic material or a moving electric charge within which the force of magnetism acts

potential energy (puh-TEN-shuhl EN-ur-jee)—energy stored within an object, waiting to be released

solution (suh-LOO-shuhn)—a mixture made of a substance that has been dissolved in another substance

static electricity (STAH-tik i-lek-TRISS-uh-tee)—the buildup of an electrical charge on the surface of an object

super cool (SOO-puhr KOOL)—to chill a liquid below its freezing point without it becoming solid

READ MORE

Adams, Tom. *Matter Matters*. Super Science. Somerville, Mass.: Candlewick Press, 2012.

Doudna, Kelly. *The Kids' Book of Simple Machines*. Minneapolis: Mighty Media Kids, 2015.

Mercer, Bobby. *Junk Drawer Physics: 50 Awesome Experiments That Don't Cost a Thing*. Chicago: Chicago Review Press, 2014.

INTERNET SITES

Use FactHound to find Internet sites related to this book:

Visit *www.facthound.com*

Just type in 9781515768876 and go.

Check out projects, games and lots more at
www.capstonekids.com

INDEX